*A Look at M*

*Rev. J. D. Pace*

ISBN: 1440468303
EAN-13: 9781440468308
Cover design by Pari Johnson

# Dedication

*This work is dedicated to my children; Tamatha, Zachary and Taunya (1970 – 1988) who, throughout my life, have been a constant source of my encouragement and enthusiasm ... all my love, Dad*

# TABLE OF CONTENTS

# A look at Messianic Judaism

## INTRODUCTION

Welcome to a brief look at the make up and character of Messianic Judaism; from its beginning to the present. It is my intention to give you a snapshot of this worldwide effort for some Gentile people to return to the Hebrew roots of their Christian faith and for some Jewish people to embrace Judaism and the Jewish Messiah Jesus of Nazareth - not to convert you or change your beliefs, but so that you might better understand its importance in the lives of those who have chosen this ancient path. I hope and pray that you will find this material thought provoking, enlightening and enjoyable.

*Blessings and much Shalom*
*Rabbi James D. Pace*

## What this book is not

- This book is not a Bible study, although I will be presenting some Scripture for your consideration.
- This book is not a Hebrew course, although I will present some Hebrew, to help you understand terminology.
- This book is not a Doctrinal presentation, although we will explore some Doctrines.
- This book is not a book to convert you or change your core beliefs, but I hope it may challenge you as we look at some different perspectives.

## Topics we will cover

- Sabbath; when and why
- History of Messianic Judaism
- Terminology
- Some Jewish Traditions and their meaning
- Messianic Organizations; the alphabet soup
- Praying and prayers
- Liturgy

**Each chapter will also suggest:**
- A little homework; weekly assignments
- Field Trips; a visit to a Messianic Congregations for Erv Sabbath or Sabbath Service

## Suggested weekly reading schedule

1. Begin each chapter with prayer.
2. Review previous homework assignments.
3. Read current chapter.
4. Develop questions and research the answers.
5. New Assignment.
6. Close your chapter study in prayer.

Although I suggest that you study one chapter per week, to give you time to absorb and consider each subject, I understand that some will wish to move at different paces. I do, however, encourage a time of prayer at the beginning and end of each study unit.

# Other Recommended Reading and Resources

| TITLE | AUTHOR |
|---|---|
| The Second Reformation | Dr. Allan Poyner |
| They Loved The Torah | David Friedman PhD |
| God's Appointed Times | Barney Kasdan |
| Bar Barakah | Craig Hill |
| The Messianic Answer Book | Sam Nadler |
| A Call to Holiness | Bruce Booker PhD |
| Expectations | Patrick Prill |
| King of the Jews | D. Thomas Lancaster |
| Messianic Services for the Festivals and Holy Days | Dr. John Fisher |
| The Complete Idiots Guide to the Talmud | Rabbi Aaron Parry |
| Webster's New World Hebrew Dictionary | |
| First Steps in Hebrew Prayer | Dr. Danny ben Gigi |

# Chapter 1: Why Messianic Judaism

For over two thousand years Christianity has run away from Judaism and Judaism has run away from Christianity. Scholars, leaders and laity of both groups have found reasons – backed by tradition or their interpretation of Scripture that justifies a particular reason for rejecting the other. How sad it is that both groups are blinded by situational influences sometimes augmented by anger and hate that go against not only the revered Torah of Judaism but the teachings of Jesus of Nazareth.

Oh we are quick to blame each other for the division; Christians say the Jewish people rejected Jesus as Messiah and the Judaism claims that although Jesus was a good person and probably a revered Rabbi, he was not the Messiah – and how could he be, when so much death and pain has been set on the world in his name
So on one side we have the Jews and on the other side we have the Christians. Both sides believing that they are correct in their interpretation of Scripture and Tradition and both sides claiming the absolute and final judgment on the Jesus matter; *He is Messiah!! He is not Messiah!!*

Caught between the two groups is a much smaller group that is as old as the argument itself. There are many names for this group; *Messianic Jews, Messianics, Members of the Hebrew Roots Movement* and other names that try to connect them to both sides of the argument, as if they were the catalyst that would make it all work … sorrowfully for the two thousand year old combatants – they may be! In the time of Jesus, the group was known by a number of names including *The Way*.

Let's begin by looking at some particular Scriptures from the Apostolic Writings

*Matthew 16:*
*¹³Now when Jesus came into the district of Caesarea Philippi, He was asking His disciples, "Who do people say that the Son of Man is?" ¹⁴And they said, "Some say John the Baptist; and others, Elijah; but still others, Jeremiah, or one of the prophets." ¹⁵He said to them, "But who do you say that I am?" ¹⁶Simon Peter answered, "You are the Christ, the Son of the living God." ¹⁷And Jesus said to him, "Blessed are you, Simon Barjona, because flesh and blood did not reveal this to you, but My Father who is in heaven. ¹⁸"I also say to you that you are Peter, and upon this rock I will build My church; and the gates of Hades will not overpower it. ¹⁹"I will give you the keys of the kingdom of heaven; and whatever you bind on earth shall have been bound in*

*heaven, and whatever you loose on earth shall have been loosed in heaven."* <sup>20</sup>*Then He warned the disciples that they should tell no one that He was the Christ (NASB)*

It would seem that from the English reading of this Scripture, it was Jesus' intention to begin a new religious movement or organization that would separate itself for Judaism, to be called "The Church". Unfortunately, this notion is far from the reality of the teaching. First of all, the word "church" was not a word of the time and did not become common use for many years to come. However, most English Translations have inserted the word "church" replacing another word that describes something quite different. *In fact, nowhere in the original texts is there any indication of Jesus establishing anything new – on the contrary He seems to be teaching a return to the original intent of God's instructions and moving away from traditions that are not grounded in Scripture.*

Let's look at another Scripture in Matthew 5:

<sup>17</sup> *"Do not think that I came to abolish the Law or the Prophets; I did not come to abolish but to fulfill.* <sup>18</sup> *"For truly I say to you, until heaven and earth pass away, not the smallest letter or stroke shall pass from the Law until all is accomplished.* <sup>19</sup> *"Whoever then annuls one of the least of these commandments, and teaches others to do the same, shall be called least in the kingdom of heaven;*

7

*but whoever keeps and teaches them, he shall be called great in the kingdom of heaven. (NASB)*

We can argue until the cows come home about the meaning of words; but here is absolute proof that Jesus was not trying to change God's commandments or get rid of the Laws that God gave Moses and the Prophets taught from – in fact Jesus clearly warns us *not* to change a thing! This passage is a clear admonition to return to God's ways and not follow some of the apostate leadership of the times, who had made up rules that shackled and put an enormous burden on the people.

And finally, from 2 John:

*[4]I was very glad to find some of your children walking in truth, just as we have received commandment to do from the Father. [5]Now I ask you, lady, not as though I were writing to you a new commandment, but the one which we have had from the beginning, that we love one another. [6]And this is love, that we walk according to His commandments. This is the commandment, just as you have heard from the beginning, that you should walk in it. (NASB)*

It is clear that the Apostle Paul, even after having been saved, is teaching that we must walk "in the truth just as we have been commanded by the Father". Jesus obeyed the Commandments of Torah; The Apostles obeyed the

Commandments of Torah; Paul obeyed the Commandments of Torah and we believe that we must endeavor to obey the Commandments of Torah. Why? Because God said to, Jesus taught us to and Paul exampled the life of Torah; and this was the way it was in the time of Jesus. There was no new church, there was no rejection of God's Commandments and not all of the Jews of that time or this, rejected Jesus as Messiah. And quite frankly, not all of the Gentiles of that time or this accepted Jesus as Messiah.

So why Messianic? Because we believe that the work first started at the time of creation, continued at Mt. Moriah, enforced in the desert of Sainai and proclaimed by Jesus of Nazareth, continues today. The Torah was *not* abolished, a new church was *not* started and God knows better than we do, what is best for our lives.

Messianic Judaism or the Hebrew Roots Movement is an attempt by many people …. beginning at the time of Jesus and continuing until today … to return to the way it was first established by the one true God of the universe.

**Chapter Assignment:** do some research on two or three Messianic Congregations in the United States. Pay close attention to their "statement of faith". Note the differences in the worship style and membership.

## Chapter 2: A Brief History

**What is Messianic Judaism?** Messianic Judaism takes various looks, throughout the world, however there are common threads weaving through most Messianic Congregations. Messianic Judaism is centered on the life and teachings of Jesus of Nazareth – who is referred to as Yeshua, his given Hebrew name. Various sources report almost 300,000 adherents to Messianic Judaism and 2500 Messianic congregations throughout the world (These numbers reflect statistics being gathered through the major Messianic Organizations, such as MJAA, UMJC and so forth, as well as the many independent Congregations).

Like Christians, and unlike the adherents to mainstream Judaism, Messianic Jews believe that Yeshua (Jesus) is the promised Messiah of the Scriptures. Most Messianic Jews identify Messianic Judaism as the natural progression and culmination of Judaism rather than a branch of Christianity – an opinion not shared by, and *vehemently* rejected by all major Jewish denominations as well as national Jewish organizations and the State of Israel.

There are a few disputes over terms that identify Messianic Believers and Messianic Congregations. Identifying terms and labels are self appointed, for the most part, and at times seem to contradict one another.

For instance to say "I'm Messianic" is a phrase that could be uttered by anyone who believes in Yeshua (Jesus) including a Baptist, Lutheran, Assemblies of God and so forth. The phrase could also be used by an Orthodox Jew as well – as Jewish people *do* believe in a Messiah – although they just don't believe that He is Jesus. For the most part, adherents to Messianic Judaism refer to themselves as Messianic Believers or Messianics.

Messianics trace their origins to the first Jewish believers in Yeshua, who called themselves *"the way"*, (Acts 9:2) but were called *Nazarenes* by the non-believing Jews and *Christians* by the non-believing Gentiles; both terms being considered derogatory at that time. For the most part, the belief in Jesus as God and Messiah falls outside the belief of mainstream Judaism, however, most historians concede that the original Nazarenes were accepted as a sect of Judaism up to the second revolt, around 132 CE/AD.

It should be noted here that during the second revolt, there was a rebel leader named Simon Bar Kochba, who rose against the Romans. Rabbi Akiva (a very famous Rabbi of the time who is quoted even today) declared that Bar Kochba was the Messiah, even though Simon had none of the accepted qualifications according to Scripture. Writer and Teacher Sam Nadler states: *"No Jewish authority has ever said Akiva is no longer a Jew for believing in a false Messiah – if after endorsing a false Messiah Akiva is still a Jew in good standing, then a Jew who believes in Yeshua as Messiah cannot be considered otherwise".*

The Nazarene believers began to pull away from the Gentile Christians after the Gentile Believers began to adopt what were seen as pagan practices, (Roman cultural activities and mores) in the second century. However it was the Council at Nicea in 325 CE where a formal declaration of division mandated a split from Jewish Believers and adopted practices for the Gentile church such as Easter instead of the High Holy Days and Passover of Judaism.

There are, today, some teachers in the Modern Church who will teach that the first followers of Yeshua were anti-Semitic in their approach to Judaism well before Constantine came to power. This teaching was and is very wrong; in fact it was Constantine who eventually legalized the anti-Jewish approach to the then known church, thus providing the preliminaries to the Niacean Council that officially divided the Believing Gentiles from the Believing Jews.

It was the Emperor's actions and the rising persecution of the Gentile Believers that eventually forced the conception of the early Christian Church. Unfortunately, these attitudes still exist today in both Synagogue and Church – the division has been emphasized for almost

2,000 years as Christianity and Judaism have taken many steps to keep each other separate. Thus, the Messianic Believers (both Jew and Gentile) are the recipients of distain and criticism from both camps.

## Modern Messianic Judaism
Throughout history, especially in the late 1800's, there have been several Messianic Synagogues established. (Traditional synagogues, where the Rabbis have become believers and lead their congregants to Messiah Yeshua). Because of their Jewish culture and lifestyle they had little to do with the Messianic Movement that was growing in Europe and especially England.

Ben Abraham Synagogue was established in London by a group that called themselves Jewish Christians. Their efforts led to more awareness of Christianity with a Jewish Background. In 1866 the Hebrew-Christian Alliance of Great Britain (HCGB) was organized and eventually planted branches throughout Europe and the United States.

The Hebrew Christian Alliance of America (HCAA) was founded in 1915 and was followed in 1925 by the International Hebrew Christian Alliance (IHCA) which later became the International Messianic Jewish Alliance. Since then many other groups have been formed to promote what has become a worldwide Messianic Movement. For the most part, the overwhelming majority of participants in these and other Congregations and Organizations were Jewish. Not many Gentiles belonged, mostly because they weren't truly accepted as "partners in the walk with Messiah".

A major shift took place in the movement in 1971 when Martin Chernoff became president of the HCAA. In 1973 a motion was made to change the name of the organization to Messianic Jewish Alliance of America (MJAA) and in 1975 the name was officially changed. At that time the two tier membership was established, allowing non-Jewish Believers to join the organization as an associate member. Since then many other organizations have been established, mainly to preserve the Jewish identity of those Jews who find Yeshua, but to promote various degrees of cooperation between Jew and Gentile Believers.

It was the organization First Fruits of Zion (FFOZ) that I believe became most influential, by inspiring many Gentile Believers to become involved in the Messianic/Hebrew Roots Movement. In the early 1990's Boaz Michael and Amber, his wife, came to an inspired conclusion that there was one Law that revealed one Covenant for Messianic Gentiles and Messianic Jews alike. This idea was and still is met with some opposition from more Jewish centered Messianic Organizations. However, FFOZ has sustained its teaching and today accounts for a large number of

Gentiles who have found the Messianic Movement and its search for the Jewish roots of the Christian faith.

David H. Stern has produced a Messianic Jewish version of the Bible called the *Complete Jewish Bible*. This work has been fairly well received in many Messianic Jewish circles, and by some Evangelical Christian Teachers. However, a slight criticism of the work is that it is a paraphrase rather than a literal translation.

In 2001, James S. Trimm brought out a New Testament translation in English that was titled the Hebrew Roots Version, reported to have been taken from original Hebrew and Aramaic texts. In 2006 Mr. Trimm added the Old Testament portions, which seems close to the presentation of the 1917 Jewish Publication Society version of the Tanach.

**Essential Doctrines**
Today, there are many Messianic congregations throughout the world. Most, but not all, seem to adhere to these important doctrines:

1. **The Holy Scriptures** include the Tanakh (the Old Testament) and the Apostolic Writings (The New Testament) as, in their original presentation, The Inspired Word of God.
2. **The unity of God** is expressed in the statement that there is only one God (Deuteronomy 6)

15

3. **Jesus (Yeshua)** is in fact the promised Messiah of Israel who came into the world as the offspring of a virgin, ministered on the earth, was crucified, buried and rose from the dead – all in fulfillment of prophecy – and today is at the right hand of the Father, preparing for His triumphant return to this world.

There are, however, different views within Messianic Judaism as to the place and importance of Torah, Baptism in the Holy Spirit and the Church, in the daily lives and beliefs of the adherents.

In recent times, Messianic Judaism seems to have spawned many different denominations, as few Congregations seem to present their beliefs in the same manner.

In Israel, for instance, there are few congregations who teach adherence to the entire Torah. In the United States and England there are many different Liturgies and methods of teaching – and some believe that the Torah is only for Jews, some believe that it is for everyone and some believe that it isn't for anyone other than those who are Jewish and live in the Land of Israel.

The history of Messianic Judaism has solid roots, but as many Christian faiths have gone, man's interpretations and perceptions of how Worship and Holiness should be observed, has moved Messianic Judaism to present a picture of something less than solidarity.

**Chapter Assignment:** Let's take a second look at Messianic Congregations; research congregations in other countries besides the United States – especially in Israel. What differences to you find? What similarities do you find?

# Chapter 3: Jewish and Messianic Organizations

Since the beginning of mankind, one thing that has remained constant is differences!  Differences have divided families, friends, nations and churches – and the irony of it all is each difference has spawned various factions that promote unity within their specific group; each thinking that it has the right idea and everyone else is not quite on the mark.

The same phenomena exists in Jewish life as well. One of the confusing issues for new adherents is … "which group should I belong to"?

Let's look at some of these groups in order to spotlight the confusion.  The following is by no means an exhaustive list or presentation of each group, but simply some highlights.

## Orthodox Judaism

Certainly the oldest division of Judaism and until the 18$^{th}$ century there was no organized difference of opinion within Judaism.  There were some differences depending on region and community boundaries; however they seemed to be limited to specific customs, practices and even dialects of Hebrew – but again, nothing significant.

Orthodox adherents believe that God gave the entire Torah at Mt. Sinai and that which has been passed down thought-out the generations not only includes the Written Law, but the Oral Law as well – which once codified is the Talmud.

The Orthodox belief is that the 613 Commandments and the rabbinical safeguards in the form of legislated Halacha (specific community rules) are binding on every Jew no matter where he lives or the constraints of the society in which he lives. *Modern society with its technology, scientific advances and medical breakthroughs, must be evaluated through Jewish principles and law. Jewish law never changes with the times, but the times change with the law!*

Orthodox Jews stress the study and importance of Torah in daily life. An Orthodox adherent will say: *Torah study is the key to Jewish survival – with Torah we will survive, without Torah; why survive?*

## Reform Judaism
Reform Judaism is fairly new in the scheme of things. Founded in the 1800's in the U.S. and established its first Rabbinical School in 1875 in Cincinnati, Ohio. It has been reported that the lavish dinner held in honor of the first graduates of the school, featured shrimp as the main course – certainly violating Biblically Kosher Laws. In 1990, it was reported that approximately 30% of Jews in the United States identified themselves with the Reform Movement.

Reform Judaism has gone through many changes over the past 100 years, from total rejection of Zionism and opposition to a Jewish Homeland, to total support of Israel.

Reform Judaism initially took the position that Biblical and Rabbinical laws of the past were not binding on the Jews of today – it was stressed that *Ritual* impedes the overall mission of Jews to bring universal morality to the world.

In recent times there seems to be a movement back toward some of the old ways: a large majority of the newly ordained Reform Rabbis are keeping Kosher and there is an ever increasing number of Reform Jews lighting Sabbath and Chanukah candles and attending Seders, as did a generation ago. There is a movement within Reform Judaism to accept the kosher laws, Sabbath and family purity as well as a belief in the Divinity of the Torah – not in the original precepts of the Reform Judaism.

**Conservative Judaism**
Conservative Judaism became a rising force of compromise under Rabbi Schecter of Columbia University in the early 1900's, and finds itself in the middle of the road between Orthodoxy and Reform. Conservatives believe in the beauty of tradition and

innovation but depart from tradition by allowing members to drive automobiles to synagogue, allow men and women to sit together in Service and has expanded the role of women in the operation of the Synagogue.

Conservative adherents take a hard stand against the main teaching of the Reform in regards to the Divinity of the Torah and some of the other practices, saying *"Serving bacon and studying Torah are not compatible"*.

**Reconstructionist Judaism**
The Reconstructionist movement was founded in the 1900's by Rabbi Mordechai Kaplan, who seemed to believe that Judaism was a culture rather than a religion. Within the movement there seems to be more of an emphasis on Jewry and culture than God and Commandments. In a bit of an interesting presentation, Reconstructionist adherents seem to place more emphasis on observance than do the Reforms.

Reconstructionist Synagogues are very involved in various local community affairs and individual rights issues. In many cities, gay rights, especially in the clergy, and other social issues have been an emphasis of many Reconstructionist communities. .

Again, let me point out that just as in Christianity, there is a wide assortment of beliefs and practices in Judaism, many of which are "man made", rather than Scriptural.

Now let's look at some of the modern day Messianic Organizations:

*Diversity in belief – Diversity in practice are the hallmarks of Judaism. Is it no wonder that the same characteristics are present in the lives and organizations of Messianic Judaism?*

**Messianic Jewish Alliance of America – MJAA**
Began in the early 1900's as Hebrew Christian Alliance of America. In the 1970's its emphasis changed and Gentile membership was offered in a two-tier system of membership.

MJAA is the largest association of Messianic Jews in the world. Its purpose is threefold:
1. To testify to the large and growing number of Jewish people who believe that Yeshua (Jesus) is the promised Jewish Messiah and Savior of the world
2. To bring together Jews and non-Jews who have a shared vision for Jewish revival
3. To introduce our Jewish brothers and sisters to the Jewish Messiah Yeshua.

MJAA sponsors conferences throughout the US each year that are usually quite large with various speakers and performers. Although MJAA has an arm for

Congregational membership, its main emphasis is individual membership. Most MJAA members attend independent Messianic Jewish congregations and synagogues. The MJAA is also affiliated with Messianic Jewish alliances in fifteen countries, including Israel.

**MJAA Statement of Faith**: *Messianic Judaism is a Biblically-based movement of people who, as committed Jews, believe in Yeshua (Jesus) as the Jewish Messiah of Israel of whom the Jewish Law and Prophets spoke.*

To many, this seems like a glaring contradiction - Christians *are Christians, Jews are decidedly not Christian.* So goes the understanding that has prevailed through nearly two thousand years of history.

Many Messianic Jews call this a mistaken - and even anti-Scriptural - understanding. Historical and Biblical evidence demonstrates that following Yeshua was initially an entirely Jewish concept. Decades upon decades of persecution, division, and confused theology have all contributed to the dichotomy between Jews and Gentile believers in Yeshua that many take for granted today.

**Union of Messianic Jewish Congregations – UMJC**
Although not heavily publicized, UMJC was a split from MJAA. A fairly large organization, we see more of an

influence in the East and Southeast regions of the US and in California.

**UMJC Statement of Purpose:** The Union of Messianic Jewish Congregations (UMJC) envisions Messianic Judaism as a movement of Jewish congregations and groups committed to Yeshua the Messiah that embrace the covenantal responsibility of Jewish life and identity rooted in Torah, expressed in tradition, and renewed and applied in the context of the New Covenant. Messianic Jewish groups may also include those from non-Jewish backgrounds who have a confirmed call to participate fully in the life and destiny of the Jewish people. We are committed to embodying this definition in our constituent congregations and in our shared institutions.

UMJC sponsors several conferences throughout the year in various Regions of the US where, as with MJAA, various speakers and performers present. Membership in UMJC is limited to Congregations in a three-tiered system.

**Messianic Israel Alliance – MIA**
Established in 1999 declare over 120 affiliated Congregations in the US and 30 more throughout the rest of the world. MIA has a multi-tiered system of membership, however makes no distinction between Jew and Gentile as their belief is that the Gentiles are expressed in the Two House/Ephraimite doctrine and the

related speculation about the 10 Northern Tribes of Israel being 'lost' and reappearing in the Diaspora. This teaching has brought a great deal of controversy among other organizations. Having spoken to many people who subscribe to the MIA position, I can assure you that although I may disagree with their stand on this issue, I consider them my sisters and brothers, for they are serious believers in Yeshua as Messiah.

**Messianic Bureau International – MBI:**
Was founded in March of 1994 by David Hargis as an information service to Messianic Judaism and is based out of Newport News, VA, USA. There are a number of chartered congregations/ministries in the United States, as well as several licensed/ordained ministers who affiliate with MBI. David Hargis was a graduate of Central Bible College, Lael University, International Seminary and Bible College and MBI Yeshiva. Hargis died December 2006 of a heart attack, but the Board is continuing on his legacy and the ministry.

THREE GREAT PILLARS OF FAITH

- The Preeminence of Messiah Yeshua: Yeshua of Nazareth is Israel's Messiah and G-d Himself who came in human flesh.
- The Permanence of Torah: All G-d's commandments and covenants continue throughout all time.

- The Promises to Israel: All the prophecies and promises which G-d gave to Israel in the Holy Scriptures will come to fruition.

---

There are several other Messianic Organizations in the United States and around the world and every once in a while, another sprouts forth – generally due to, once again, man determining that the previous organization doesn't have it quite right! I must say that regardless of the differences in each organization, I believe that there is a common thread of *love for the God of the Universe and the Messiah of the world, which* runs through them all.

I will close with a quote from Steve Shermett of AMC on the matter of the relationship between Gentile and Jewish adherents to Messianic Judaism:

*"Gentile Believers in Messiah Yeshua are beloved of God and do not need to invent, imagine or make up a false Jewish/Hebrew/Israel lineage to be top-ranked "players" in the family of God. God loves Gentiles who love the Messiah"*

**Chapter Assignment:** Find a Messianic Congregation in your area and attend a service. Note the similarities and differences between the Messianic service and the church or synagogue service you have experienced in the past. Ask the leadership if they belong to or are affiliated with any of the Messianic Organizations.

# Chapter 4: Sabbath & Festivals

One of the most distinguishing characteristics of Messianic Judaism is the observance of the Sabbath. Unlike most of Christianity, Judaism (including Messianic Judaism) believes that the "seventh day" is day set apart by God as the Sabbath. Mistakenly, much of the modern church believes that the story in Acts 20:7 was a "divine indication" that God had changed the day of Sabbath from Saturday (the 7th day) to Sunday (the 1[rst] day). This, of course, is not the point of the story and certainly there was not an official change until the 4th century when the Roman Church began the practice of meeting on Sunday. Nevertheless, the Sabbath has always been and will always be the 7th day of the week – which coincides with what we know as Saturday.

A search of the New Revised Standard Translation shows 157 citations about the Sabbath; from the establishment of Sabbath in Genesis 1 to Hebrews 4:9 that says: *[9]So then, a Sabbath rest still remains for the people of God.*

At no time and in no Scripture will you find that Sabbath has changed from the 7th day to the 1rst day of the week … nor will you find that Sabbath has been replaced by "the Lord's day" – a common term used to refer to Sunday.

Thomas LaMance, a contemporary French author, writes: *"Life is what happens to us while we are making other plans"*. How true it is! Unfortunately, life happens too fast for most of us; and before you know it …many years have passed us by. This is driven home most poignantly with the growth of a child. One moment they are babies and the next they are grown and have families of their own. Before we know it, life is over. Rabbi Blech put it this way: "Life can be summed up in three words: *hurry, worry and bury"*. The Sabbath has been given to us so that for a short time, we can step away from the fast-tempo living of the rest of the week.

Sabbath has been discussed and discussed, especially the "rules of Sabbath", for centuries. What should we do, how should we act, what should we wear, how do we get around/travel, how can we stay warm? And the questions go on and on.

There are Scriptural rules of Sabbath: *Don't do any work or ordinary work, don't kindle a fire, don't put a burden on others* and so forth. In order to keep us from breaking the Scriptural rules – man has devised other rules called "fences" that keep us at a distance. For instance, we are not to kindle a fire on Sabbath. In order that we might not accidentally break this rule, Some Orthodox Jews will not turn on a electric light or drive a car. There are some appliance manufacturers that make stoves that can be programmed not to come on, on the Sabbath;

Refrigerators and Freezers that will not allow the light, inside, to come on when you open the door – even the motors that run the compressor will not turn on during the Sabbath. Some homes, especially in Israel, have timers that shut the power off to the home just before the Sabbath begins and turn it back on just after the Sabbath ends.

It would seem that there is more work to observing Sabbath than not! Remembering all the rules and putting them into practice would certainly be a chore, unless one was familiar with the rules due to growing up with them.. Sometimes, I think mankind misses the point of the Sabbath.

Abraham Herschel, a twentieth century theologian, said of the Sabbath: *"The Temple was a sanctuary in space; the Sabbath is a sanctuary in time. For six days we live our life on the level of "how"; every seventh day we change the focus of our existence to "why".*

Sabbath should never be a burden to us, but a Blessing.. Our Messiah was complaining about the way people treated the Sabbath in Mark 2:27 when He said that Sabbath was made for man!

*[23] And it happened that He was passing through the grain fields on the Sabbath, and His disciples began to make their way along while picking the heads of grain. [24] The Pharisees*

*were saying to Him, "Look, why are they doing what is not lawful on the Sabbath?"* [25]*And He said to them, "Have you never read what David did when he was in need and he and his companions became hungry;* [26]*how he entered the house of God in the time of Abiathar the high priest, and ate the consecrated bread, which is not lawful for anyone to eat except the priests, and he also gave it to those who were with him?"* [27]***Jesus said to them,*** *"The Sabbath was made for man, and not man for the Sabbath.* [28]*"So the Son of Man is Lord even of the Sabbath." (NASB)*

And then we see from Exodus:

[9]*Six days you shall labor and do all your work.* [10]*But the seventh day is a Sabbath to the LORD your God; you shall not do any work—you, your son or your daughter, your male or female slave, your livestock, or the alien resident in your towns.* [11]*For in six days the LORD made heaven and earth, the sea, and all that is in them, but rested the seventh day; therefore the LORD blessed the Sabbath day and consecrated it. (Exodus 20)*

It is clear that God intended the 7th day to be very special … not full of rules and regulations that would bog us down. Sabbath should be a day to get in touch with God, to rest in His wonderfulness and to spend time with your family.

Sabbath should allow us the time to rediscover our family and friends. Some Orthodox Jews won't even answer the phone or turn on the television, on Sabbath. It should be a time to ESCAPE from the mundane and profane and a time to be involved in the world of the sacred. Sabbath should allow us to find the time to talk, to sing, to feast, to pray, to study and even have close personal relationships with our spouse -which is a Mitzvah - on Friday night. Can you ask for a more perfect way to spend a day?

In order to have our Sabbaths to become a special time of spiritual and physical delight, tradition recommends some specific activities for Sabbath:

- Eat three meals on Sabbath
- Sing special and Joyful songs with our family
- Wear our finest clothes
- Spend time with your family
- Spend time in prayer in Synagogue
- Do not talk about the past week
- Review and renew the direction of your lives

Sabbath should be a time to pray Blessings on each other, a happy time, a time to draw close to our loved ones and the One who loved us first.

Eric Fromm, not one of my favorite authors due to his liberal views, once said: *"The Sabbath is the day of complete harmony between man and nature. Work is any kind of disturbance of the man-nature equilibrium. By not working – that is to say by not participating in the process of actual and social change – man is free from the chains of time".*

_____

The Festivals of our God are, once again, special to those who are Jewish and those who belong to Messianic Congregations. These are God's appointed times, which He says we should observe *in every generation!* Leviticus 23:1, talks about the Sabbath and the Festivals:

*[1]The LORD spoke again to Moses, saying, [2]"Speak to the sons of Israel and say to them, 'The LORD'S appointed times which you shall proclaim as holy convocations— My appointed times are these:*
*[3]'For six days work may be done, but on the seventh day there is a sabbath of complete rest, a holy convocation. You shall not do any work; it is a sabbath to the LORD in all your dwellings.*
*[4]'These are the appointed times of the LORD, holy convocations which you shall proclaim at the times appointed for them. [5]'In the first month, on the fourteenth day of the month at twilight is the LORD'S Passover. [6]'Then on the fifteenth day of the same month there is the Feast of Unleavened Bread to the LORD; for seven days you shall eat unleavened bread. [7]'On the first day you shall have a holy convocation; you shall not do any laborious work. [8]'But for seven days you shall*

*present an offering by fire to the LORD. On the seventh day is a holy convocation; you shall not do any laborious work.'" (NASB)*

And reading on we will see other Festivals of the Lord, which He commanded us to observe. These are to be Holy Convocations – to be set aside from the other days of the year. The Day of Atonement, the first day of each month (in the Hebrew Calendar), the Feast of Booths, Pentecost and the other observances prescribed by Scripture are to be observed *forever or in every generation*, as our God Commanded. There are a few other observances, two of which are Purim (to remember the acts of Queen Esther) and Chanukah, (to remember the rededication of the Temple), which although not commanded by God, have been established by the people as perpetual observances, (in the same manner as Christmas and Easter were established by the Catholic church) in order that we might not forget the other important events in the history of Judaism and Christianity. Even Jesus observed Chanukah … for instance: John 10:22

*[22]At that time the Feast of the Dedication took place at Jerusalem; [23]it was winter, and Jesus was walking in the temple in the portico of Solomon.*

In Hebrew, the word for "dedication" is "Chanukah". So Jesus was observing the *Feast of Dedication or Chanukah.*

Much more can be written about the special days of God, but I will refer you to an excellent book on the matter: *God's Appointed Times* by Barney Kasdan.

**Chapter Assignment**: Begin this next Sabbath with candle lighting and blessings and a wonderful and joyful meal with family and friends. During the Sabbath do not think of the past week, but focus on your loved ones and on the One who first loved you. Make this Sabbath different than any of the ones in the past – maybe you will begin a new tradition in your family.. At all times, remember that Sabbath was made for YOU, not YOU for Sabbath

As part of your observance of Sabbath, here are some suggestions of blessings that you might use; or use your own prayers to accomplish the same.

First Blessing – Lighting the Candles (usually done by a woman)

As you light the candles say: *Blessed are you O Lord our God, who has taught us your ways through the Holy Scriptures and has inspired us to light the Sabbath lights.*

Now take some time to say a blessing over each other and don't forget your children. Say a blessing over the food and then enjoy the evening.

Finally, when you are finished with your meal and fellowship, thank God for the blessings that he has showered upon you.

# Chapter 5: What is food?

In the previous chapter we discussed one of the principal characteristics of Messianic Judaism, that makes us different from the contemporary church, as being the Sabbath; following close behind is of course kosher food. **"Jesus changed the rules of what we eat" and "God changed the rule for what we eat in Peter's vision"** are two of the most common proclamations in response to our desire to eat kosher. Let's explore some food issues.

Owen Meredith, a 19th century English Poet wrote:

*We may live without poetry, music and art;*
*We may live without conscience and live without heart;*
*We may live without friends, we may live without books*
*But civilized man cannot live without cooks!*

Around my house and maybe yours, the kitchen is one of the most important rooms in the home. I remember growing up and experiencing the smells, the warmth and the conversations that took place in the kitchen – it was wonderful. It was not hard to figure out the importance of the kitchen; Rabbi Blech says it is the source of our daily bread!

Food seems to be important to God as well. If it wasn't, then why did He give us the rules that *should* govern our food? *The Midrash Leviticus Rabbah says "A physician*

*restricts the diet of only those patients whom he expects
to recover. So God prescribed dietary laws for those
who have hope for a future life – others may eat
anything"*

Contrary to some popular thought, kosher food isn't food
blessed by the Rabbi. Some people must think that if the
Catholic Priest blesses the water to make it Holy Water,
Rabbis must do something similar. Another
misconception is that kosher food is somehow the
definition of SUPER CLEAN FOOD. *If it were only so.*

The word kosher means "fit or suitable "– which can
actually apply to other things besides food. On the
matter of food, it means *food that is acceptable by Jewish
Law.* What ultimately makes it kosher is its approval by
the Highest Authority of all and codified in His
Scriptures.

Here is another misconception in regards to kosher food:
**Kosher food laws are based on health issues and are
meant to prevent sickness.** Well, although I believe that
it is healthier to eat kosher rather than non-kosher, there
is nothing in the Torah that indicates that this was the
intention of God. Of course over the years modern
science has proven that a kosher diet is much healthier
than a non kosher one … but even so, people ignore what
is best for them. I think God knew and still knows what
is best for us. Don't You?

So why eat kosher? First and foremost because God said to eat kosher; a secondary answer is that kosher is better for you!

Moses Maimonides, in his "Guide for the Perplexed" says: *Dietary laws train us to master our appetites and not to consider eating and drinking the end of man's existence.* Jewish Philosophers agree that kosher diet laws teach us self control, and have a direct effect on our urges to participate in other things that are not good for us.

Scholars point out that under Jewish Law, permissible animals are all herbivorous – they eat plants; and the not permitted animals will eat meat.

Think about it; what did Adam and Eve eat in the Garden?

**[16]And the Lord God commanded the man, saying, "Of every tree of the garden you may freely eat; [17]but of the tree of the knowledge of good and evil you shall not eat, for in the day that you eat of it you shall surely die." (Genesis 2:16)**

Were there animals in the garden? Yes. Did they eat them? We don't think so. Did they eat of the forbidden tree? Yes. What happened?

There are consequences for disobeying what God has commanded us … even regarding food.

Well, *we* can eat some animals: Those that have a split hoof and chew a cud. I'm not sure what the issue is with the hoof, but animals that chew a cud eat what? Vegetation! So we can eat: cattle, sheep, goats, deer and other animals that meet the qualification. But watch out! There are some wolves in sheep's clothing!

The Pig has a split hoof … but doesn't chew a cud. In fact a pig will eat just about anything you put before it.

Isn't that like a lot of sin? The pig looks kosher on the outside, but on the inside he certainly isn't kosher. Sin can look good on the outside, but on the inside is certainly not kosher.

There is much more to say about the foods we can or can not eat. There are books and lists of clean and unclean foods; find one and keep it close to your kitchen

A few more comments on kosher: As I said before, kosher can apply to other things besides food. For one thing, it applies to the way animals are slaughtered. My Grandfather was the most gentle of men, when it came time to butcher animals. He was skilled in the kosher ways of slaughter; his knife was extremely sharp with no nicks or dull spots, his draw was swift and sure ... as far as I know, no animal ever suffered because of my Grandfather. He was merciful in his actions. I remember him really scolding a man who tried to slaughter a cow and left it bellowing and writhing on the ground, because he cut the jugular but not the vagus nerve.

Research has taught us that Kosher Slaughtering results in instant loss of consciousness. The cut itself is fairly painless, much like being cut with a razor blade.

Jews are not permitted to eat blood. So, slaughtered meat is soaked in a salt water solution prior to being cooked – or at a processing plant. The blood and impurities are drained off ... then the meat is ready for seasoning, cooking and eating.

You see, to be kosher food, there is much more involved other than which list it came from.

One last comment: Food that is not healthy is probably not kosher. Kosher food *is* good for you – unless you have a specific allergy to a specific food or if you are on a very restricted diet. We must be smart about what we eat; we must accept that God knows better than we as to what is good for us, and we must accept the fact that He would not have us eat anything that isn't good for us.

**Chapter Assignment:** Have a kosher meal with your family and discuss what the menu was, how it was prepared and how you liked it. Consider the healthiness of eating kosher. Do you think that God knew what He was doing when He set down the dietary laws?

# Chapter 6: Prayer

Christians, Jews, Muslim and just about any religious group on the face of the earth will eventually find themselves in prayer. Even those who claim to be atheists will exclaim thanks to the Creator of the Universe, when they are saved from some disaster – then they will get red in the face. It has been reported that in the middle of a "separation of church and state" argument between Madelyn O'Hara and her detractors, she exclaimed "Thank God I'm an atheist"!

Our forefathers spoke much about the importance of praying. They taught that an individual needs to spend time in prayer … connecting with our God and opening ourselves to hear His response and revelation.

Nobody can explain it in generally accepted terms, but some scientists are stumped at the concept that prayer works; people who pray get better faster, people whom others pray for, even when they are unaware of the prayers, recover at a greater rate. Do you understand how important and powerful prayer is?

As you might imagine, questions arise, often, in regards to prayer (usually from non-believers … but sometimes believers) that challenge the need for prayer:

- Is God such an egotist that He has to hear us praise Him?
- If I am bringing my problems to God by praying, does that mean He hasn't been paying attention to me?
- Protestant Harry Emerson Fosdick asks "Is God a cosmic bellhop who waits for us to place our order"?
- If we truly believe that God is capable of running the world according to His will, isn't prayer the ultimate act of arrogance – asking Him to change His mind?

Jewish Sages answer these and other question by explaining that prayer isn't meant to *change God*; it is meant to *change us!* Prayer is not supposed to save us, it is to make us worth saving.

The word prayer (in English) comes from a Greek root PRECARE, which means to beg. Rabbis teach that to beg God is not the point of prayer. In Hebrew the phrase "to pray" can be transliterated L'Hitpallel – which can mean TO STAND IN SELF-JUDGEMENT. As we pray, we should be raising our understanding and awareness of God. Standing in His presence, we should begin to feel different; possibly more spiritual but most assuredly we should be finding ourselves improving in the way that we react to God's will and to His other children around us.

We should become, hopefully, a better person who will be Blessed of God; which is one way we have our prayers answered.

In Judaism there are three words that describe three different kinds of prayre:

1. Shevach – prayers of praise
2. Bakashah – prayers of request
3. Hodaah – prayers of thanksgiving

In all of these forms of prayer we should be awakened to the Awesomeness of our God and His Majesty. To forget any of these is to forget them all.

The Jewish Sages spoke about the importance of praying in Hebrew. They have taught that although it was permitted to pray in the vernacular of our societies, Hebrew was always favored. Lashon HaKodesh (the Holy tongue) was the language of our forefathers and the language of our God.

Yeshua (Jesus) spoke to the importance and character of prayer in Matthew 6:5

*5 "And whenever you pray, do not be like the hypocrites; for they love to stand and pray in the synagogues and at the street corners, so that they may be seen by others. Truly I tell you, they have received their reward. 6But*

45

*whenever you pray, go into your room and shut the door and pray to your Father who is in secret; and your Father who sees in secret will reward you.*
*[7]"When you are praying, do not heap up empty phrases as the Gentiles do; for they think that they will be heard because of their many words. [8]Do not be like them, for your Father knows what you need before you ask him.*

In his seminar, *First Steps in Hebrew Prayer*, Danny Ben Gigi talks about the importance of praying in Hebrew, but emphasizes that knowing the meaning of the Hebrew words that you say is critical to experience the fullness of prayer. Some of the Sages have taught that it is better to pray in Hebrew – even if you don't understand the words, but I would suggest that it is so much a better experience if you do understand.

There are many sources of prayers in various prayer books. www.artscroll.com is a great source of many different Siddurim (prayer books). You can find prayer books in many languages including Hebrew/English. I recommend that you all have at least one for your personal use..

Let's learn a simple prayer, first in English, then in Hebrew.

**Chapter Assignment**: Learn this traditional Morning Prayer in English and in Hebrew:

(The Hebrew words are transliterated)

MO-DEH (FEMALES SAY MO-DAH) A-NI LE FA NE
CHA
I greatefully thank you
ME-LECH CHAI VE-KA-YAM
Living and existing King
SHE-HE-CHE-ZAR-TA BEE NISN-MA-TI BE-CHEM-
LA
For returning my soul within me with compassion
RA-BA E-MU-NA-TE-CHA
Abundant is Your faithfulness

# Chapter 7: Liturgy

A liturgy is the customary public worship done by a specific religious group, according to their particular traditions. The word may refer to an elaborate formal ritual such as the Eastern Orthodox Divine Liturgy and Catholic Mass, or a daily activity such as the Muslim Salat and Jewish Shacharit. In most Christian circles, churches may be designated 'Liturgical' or 'Non-Liturgical' churches, depending on how formal or elaborate their Services are. I think possibly that there is in error in this thinking here, for regardless of the church – if there is a normal and pre-set 'order of service' ... I believe that order becomes Liturgy.

Although the word Liturgy seems to come from a Greek word *leitourgia* which literally means *Public Work,* and often referred to some public work for the good of the community done by a wealthy person, the church seems to have taken *its* use from the Greek text of the Apostolic writings such as Acts 13:2.
*²While they were ministering to the Lord and fasting, the Holy Spirit said, "Set apart for Me Barnabas and Saul for the work to which I have called them." ³Then, when they had fasted and prayed and laid their hands on them, they sent them away. (NASB)*

The foregoing verse seems to point to a well-defined and public act known by the community. Although the word Liturgy seems to address *public worship or ministry*, (words that are sometimes interchanged with liturgy) the Byzantine Rite places the word 'Divine' prior to the word Liturgy to indicate a Eucharistic or Communion Service, in which only the members of their sect are permitted to participate.

In Messianic Judaism, there are many forms of Liturgy. From the very Orthodox style of Liturgy that might be found in a Synagogue to the Liturgy of a modern Evangelical church. Each form helps define the specific community for which it was developed and guides them in their Worship of God on Sabbath and other observed events of the Liturgical Calendar.

Various Liturgies can be found in some Siddurim (Prayer Books) that have been specifically designed for Messianic Congregations. Dr. John Fisher and Cantor Jeremiah Greenburg have both developed the most used Messianic Siddurim for Sabbath. Both of these works present specific Liturgy which also includes prayers and references to Jesus our Messiah - such references would not be found in mainstream Judaism. There are a host of other Messianic writers who have developed specific Siddurim for various Messianic Congregations – many of which can be found on the Internet.

49

No one Congregation or writer can take credit for the best or *most Messianic* Siddur. What works in one community does not necessarily work in the next. Unfortunately, this phenomena causes difficulties within communities, especially when someone joins the community, having been in or visited another community, and insisting that the other way is the best.

Virtually all Siddurim I have seen for Congregations in the United States will present a Liturgy in Hebrew (usually by way of transliteration) and always with English translations; and in most Congregations both the Hebrew and English are read. Most people in the United States do not speak or read Hebrew, so this accommodation is important and often inspires people to actually learn some Hebrew. Another concept of these works is their insistence on a mixture of traditional prayers and the inclusion of references to Jesus as the promised Messiah.

We know that Liturgy by itself can not save a soul; but it can help a person to focus their thoughts on the One who should be Worshiped, Blessed be He. We also know that if is difficult for some people to initially participate in a Liturgical Worship Service when they have had no pervious exposure to such formal traditions. Finally, we know that *change* is difficult for many people and to change to a formal Liturgy can be intimidating. (The only people who like change are babies and bus drivers)

The successful Messianic Congregations take these issues into consideration and with love and compassion help visitors and new members adjust to a beautiful way to focus our Worship on the God of the Universe, who created all.

**Chapter Assignment:** Try to visit a Messianic Congregation in your area or a Liturgical Church. Go with an open mind and a sense of adventure to experience a new way of Worship.

# Chapter 8: Tidbits when visiting

On your first visit to a Messianic Congregation, you may find some strange customs, dress and language being used by the regular attendees. Don't worry about what you see or hear and don't be afraid to ask questions. Just remember, as in any church, you may get two different answers from two different people.

First let's talk about some words you may encounter on your visit:

**Adonai:** One of the more common names for God. Generally it is used to represent the Jewish conception of the divine nature, and of the relation of God to the Jewish people.

**Challah:** is a special braided bread eaten on the Sabbath and holidays.

**Kippah:** A man's head covering – it looks like a small beanie.

**Oneg:** A time of food and fellowship following the Sabbath Service. Oneg means 'delight' and we wish to make our Sabbath a delight for ourselves and those who are visiting.

**Shabbat:** Hebrew for Sabbath, the 7<sup>th</sup> day of the week which God said to keep holy.

**Shabbat Shalom:** A traditional greeting wishing you a "Sabbath Peace".

**Shema:** *Shema Yisrael* (or Sh'ma Yisrael or just Shema ; "Hear, O Israel" are the first two words of a section of the Torah that is a centerpiece of the morning and evening Jewish prayer services. (Shema can be found in Duet. 6.

**Shul:** Actually a Yiddish word, which is derived from a German word meaning "school," and emphasizes the synagogue's role as a place of study.
**Synagogue:** A special designated place where the faith community gathers; sometimes referred to as a Jewish Church.

**Siddur:** A Prayer Book

**Tallit:** A man's prayer shawl worn by men for Morning Prayer and in Synagogue on Sabbath and most Holidays.

**Tzitzi:** Tassels that God commanded to be worn: *You shall make yourself tassels on the four corners of your garment with which you cover yourself. (Duet. 22:12 NASB)*

**Torah:** Refers to the first five books of the Bible. Unfortunately, the word Torah has been mistranslated as Law, in a number of places in the Apostolic Writings. Torah is much more than Law. The word Greek word *nomos,* instead of Law might have been better translated as Instructions.

**Yeshua:** The Hebrew name given to Jesus by his mother

---

Now let's look at some of the various things you might see being worn at a Messianic Service.

The first thing may be various types of head coverings, both by men and women. Men may be wearing Kippahs (skull caps) of various colors and designs and women may be wearing beautiful hats or scarves.

The way we dress and look matters. It sends messages to everyone else and OURSELVES about us. Halachah, Jewish Law, has rules about how Jews traditionally dress. These daily practices help identify them as Jews. However, the head covering for men and women is more than identification; we cover our heads to remind us that our God is our covering.

At the Congregation I attend, it is not mandatory for head covering. Each person will find their own level of understanding, on their own. When reading Torah I prefer that all - men and women - cover their heads as a sign of respect and submission to God and His Word.

Next, you may see some men wearing Tallits (Prayer Shawls). These Shawls come in various sizes and colors. Sometimes they will be worn around the shoulders and sometimes you may see them covering the man's head as well. The Tallit is generally worn *only* in the morning for prayer and at Shul for morning Sabbath Service or Holiday Service. The Tallit is usually not worn at night and not worn while eating and never when in the restroom.

There is much controversy over the issue of women wearing Tallit. Women began wearing Tallit only very recently with the creation of the Reform and Conservative Movements. Originally the Tallit was a kind of cloak that looked like a blanket and was worn by men in ancient times, probably resembling the abbayah ("blanket") still worn by Bedouin for protection against the weather. At the four corners of the Tallit fringes were attached in fulfillment of the biblical commandment of tzitzi (Num. 15:38-41). After the exile of the Jews from Israel the Tallit was discarded as a daily habit and it became a religious garment for prayer; hence its later meaning of prayer shawl worn by men at time of prayer.

Some of the Sages taught that women were exempt from wearing Tiztzi and therefore would not generally wear a Tallit. Additionally, some believe that the Tallit as we know it today is a man's garment and therefore would not be proper attire for women.

Deuteronomy 22:5: *"A woman shall not wear man's clothing, nor shall a man put on a woman's clothing; for whoever does these things is an abomination to the LORD your God. (NASB)*

This being said, I have seen some very beautiful women's prayer shawls – that at first glance one would know that it is a woman's garment.

In many Messianic Congregations, you may see a Torah Scroll; in fact it might be paraded through the congregation. You will see various acts of respect as the Scroll passes by. Some will reach out and touch the Scroll with a Bible or prayer book; some will kiss their fingers and touch the Scroll; some men who are wearing Tallit will take hold of one of the Tiztzi on their Tallit, kiss it and touch the Scroll with the Tiztzi. No matter what is done, the entire Congregation will follow the Scroll around the Shul with their eyes, never turning their back on the Scroll as it is paraded. The symbolism here is first a loving reverence for the Word of God and as we watch the Scroll we are saying that *we will never turn our back on the Word of God.*

Various Congregations may have various traditions before, during and after their Sabbath Services. Remember, you are welcome in our midst and your comfort and peace is important to us. Participate as much as you wish, take in the tapestry of sound and sight that has its roots in the history of mankind. Don't forget to ask questions and we hope you will find time in your busy life to visit again, or join us in this wonderful expression of Messianic Judaism.

# Epilogue

It is my hope and prayer that this book has helped you understand a bit more about some of your family, friends and neighbors who may have decided to connect to Messianic Judaism. Now you know that they haven't lost their minds and are not participating in a cult or anything that is going to send them to hell. They are people who Love God and Love Jesus; they have a deep desire to connect to the way it was in the beginning and follow the paths that were set by our God.

Messianic Judaism has a wonderful place in the architecture of our God, along with the many other different styles of Worship. It is, however, my opinion that God Himself has given His entire Scripture to show us the way we should live; and within that Scripture is a *perfect plan for our lives and a perfect plan for our Salvation.* When I look at the history of Christianity, I wonder if God ever dealt with man's burning desire to change things, by saying to us "do you really think I need your help in deciding what is best for you"? I often think of the words to the Prophet in Job 38:4

> *"Where were you when I laid the foundation of the earth?*
> *Tell Me, if you have understanding,*
> <sup>5</sup> *Who set its measurements? Since you know.*

*Or who stretched the line on it?*
*6 "On what were its bases sunk?*
*Or who laid its cornerstone,*
*7 When the morning stars sang together*
*And all the sons of God shouted for joy?(NASB)*

May God bless us for our attempts to get closer to Him and may we learn through diligent pursuit, that the Ways of God, the "ancient paths", are the best way for us to live.

***Thus says the LORD,***
***"Stand by the ways and see and ask for the ancient paths,***
***Where the good way is, and walk in it;***
***And you will find rest for your souls. (Jeremiah 6 :16 NASB)***

Made in the USA